# CONCRETE AND WILD CARROT

## MARGARET AVISON

Other Works by Margaret Avison

*Winter Sun*, 1960
*The Dumbfounding*, 1966
*sunblue*, 1978
*Winter Sun/The Dumbfounding*, 1982
*No Time*, 1989
*Selected Poems*, 1991
*Not Yet But Still*, 1997
*A Kind of Perseverance*, 1993 (Pascal Lectures at the
        University of Waterloo)


Collaborations:

*The Plough and the Pen*, 1963
*Acta Sanctorum*, 1966

# Concrete and Wild Carrot

## Margaret Avison

Brick Books

National Library of Canada Cataloguing in Publication

Avison, Margaret, 1918-
        Concrete and wild carrot / Margaret Avison

Poems.
ISBN 1-894078-24-1

        I. Title

PS8501.V5C65 2002        C811'.54        C2002-902871-X
PR9199.3.A92C65 2002

We acknowledge the support of the Canada Council for
the Arts, the Government of Canada through the Book
Publishing Industry Development Program (BPIDP),
and the Ontario Arts Council for their support of our
publishing program.

The cover photograph was taken by Paul Best.
The photograph of the author was taken by Joan Eichner.

The book is set in Bodoni and Frutiger.

Design and layout by Alan Siu.

Printed and bound by Sunville Printco Inc.

Brick Books
431 Boler Road, Box 20081
London, Ontario   N6K 4G6

brick.books@sympatico.ca

# Contents

# Pacing the Turn of the Year

A sudden season
has changed our world.
Everybody is out
to see, or bask, or
with their kind to exuberate.

Everything is new.

Trees that were only sticks
into the overcast
yesterday, are
soft and full of catkins
like newly shampooed children being
readied for the party.

Slender young saplings
shine, all the tender leaves
distinct, notes of music
atremble for a chance musician
strolling by to hear and
play — for everybody, on bikes
or park benches or
wandering along
      the way
      the city buses, dazed,
      wended their way anywhere

on the odd quiet morning
the European War
was somehow ended; nobody
felt like cavorting, singing,
dancing, as their parents, 1918,
in November, had.

A muted celebration
this sudden season.
All but the oak.

Rusty tatters left from far-off August's
leafy towers and gables,
the deeps and fullness, the amassing
in gloom and shadow of

greenness; now
ruined arthritic knobs and wrenched
limbs; next to nothing now
covering his nakedness.

The new is going to last?
These celebrants
toss their curls and
rollerblade past
the question.

It was not posed by the
dour oaks,

stolider even than
     the firs, their shabby
     winter wear refurbished
     at the tips,
standing there woodenly under
scrambling squirrels, a warm bath of
sunshine, thunderstorm,
by turns.

Part of a celebration
is to discover
patience? and how
painful hope can be?

Alone, and mute stands
dark, one huge oak tree.

## Present from Ted

It must have been after a
birthday; at Christmastime
daylight hasn't the lambency
I remember as part of
the puzzling present somebody
had given me: a scribbler, empty pages, but
not for scribbling in.
Instead of a pencil box there was
a jellyglass set out, with water, and
a brand-new paint brush.

The paper was not pretty.
A pencil-point might in an upstroke
accidentally jab a hole in it.

But, painting it —
as I was told to, with only
clear water, "Behold!"
my whole being sang out, for "see"
would not have been adequate.

The pictures that emerged
were outlines? I remember
only the paper, and the wonder of it,
and how each page was turning out to be
a different picture.

There were no colours, were there?

In the analogy, there are
glorious colours
and, in some way that lacks
equivalents,
deepening colours, patterns that keep
emerging, always
more to anticipate.

For that there is no other process.

Locked in the picture is
missing the quality of the analogy of
morning light
and the delighted holder of the paint-brush
and who gave him the book, and where he found it.

## Towards the Next Change

Leaf on the shrub
let the flow
along the corridors of a
breathing stem
ease to a trickle.

       THE SHRUB: Look for
       no energy now. You're letting in
       the cold!
       My stiffened fingers are
       icy.

                 The leaf
sighs and separates itself and
wavers away.

# Prairie Poem
*For George Grant*


To go from white-water rivers' valleys or
from the escarpment to
live on the Saskatchewan prairie is
choosing to find out that
space calls, to a reshaping
of person. This is above and
beyond the going to, the choosing.

Reading in the open world of
this writer's geography of
ideas is to look, staggered and
overwhelmed by the
ideas, almost lost in the
panorama of
the living, long-dead, to him
present as friends, each lifted face
featured for horizons. For
holding close an everywhere of sky.

The land, the books, can never
swallow you, nor even the
furry spring crocus here — however
small, at vanishing  points.

## Dividing Goods

They say it's wrong to
push a parable.
Figures of speech are still
themselves responsible for
their tendrils — though these stray.
Words have their life too, won't
compact into a theorem.

Take the story of the Prodigal Son:
an invisible third son is not mentioned,
yet he had it all
had prized it all
wanted all of it
for all so
had himself to leave
it, all.
But this one is the only
visible one. He
tells the family's story,
a simple tale but
somehow unresolved so that
its tendrils cling timelessly.

Through his eyes we see
pathos in their wanting something else.

Fool's gold restores
a starveling's taste for
a healthy meal of bread, at home;

or, (the older brother)
wanting something —
because deserving more than
this dogged servitude?

(Yet from the outset
the "mine," the "portion that is mine"
had to be less than all.)

All those were
dear to the one who

owns and gives and
loves on.

# Ramsden

Let's go to the park where
the dogs and children
cluster and circle and run
under the sombre old trees — they are
hanging on to their swarthing
leaves — while the young
medallioned trees in the early
sun are dancing
among them.
The knapsacked students too
hurtle, always too late, focused
on there, blindingly
swerving out of the now and
here where children and dogs
and a few rather shabby, slow
old ones, straying, move
across the owners, standing with
loose leashes, intent on "their day."
The benched but sleepless
mothers and nannies, watching,
are quieted here, warmed and fed
by the good old trees and
the shining little ones.

# Balancing Out

He smells of — what?
It's like wet coal-dust.
He came very late:
tangled brown hair, his face
streaked, and bleary;
no gloves, but (Merry
Christmas) from a mission, twice
blest — a good warm coat
that could go anywhere — and had!
now puckered, snagged, hem spread
from sleeping out, and ripped
around one leather elbow,
and buttoned crooked. There were no
other buttons now. He slept
there in his pew.

The giver of his topcoat eerily
watched, her widow's desolation clearly
inconsolable now
(a pang — like joy!),
to see what she had seen
on a fine, and steady man
made come full circle on this ruined fellow.

Still, he had his coat,
and she, the echoing years.

## The Crux

Ever see somebody hit bedrock
too messed up to
say so too
hopeless a mess to get his chin
far enough off the ground to
even give in?
deadbeat?

Know what that's like yourself?

Now can you credit
anyone figuring he had to
steer his fair steady days and nights
deliberately
to some as yet (I'm guessing)
point of light beyond that
abysmal (other people's) living
end?
right down, past, the dead end
to the worst? There wasn't
a "Lamb of God" for the
then lamb the wolf had torn.
But    there    gleamed
the point.

Ever see a child in his
highchair twisting with the
urgency of now, not knowing how
or what, only the
pangs, the poignancy
of *Don't you see*
*that I need everything*
*right now?*

He hears help coming.
Hope stills the moment.
Eagerness drums with heels and spoon
in a blissful lurch
towards all tomorrow.

The one the radiance touched
does see
and smile there, in that kitchen.
The point.

# Ambivalence

When the shutters are down
the outside work is pleasanter
even when fingers out of the mitts
go numb on the hammer;
the boathouse whispered with
ice-splinters and slush when I fetched the ladder.
We'll have to deal with the chimney
before we can warm the place up
inside, and then the cleaning out and sweeping up
will be dirty jobs before it's safe
to light the kindling, inside.

> After the shutters are up
> let's build a fire
> out here: there's wood
> under the cottage; we can
> open the thermos and eat our lunch
> before we tackle the rest?
> It's pleasurable outside.

Being inside will be good when we're
in and out all the time. It can be cosy
when rain is drumming the roof — but that
fireplace sometimes smokes.
In mid-July
it's stifling under the shingles

even after a midnight swim.
On such a night it is pleasanter
under the stars, outside.

> We've never been here when it's
> outside only wherever you might
> need to be to do
> whatever needed doing —
> after the local wood-and-ice fellow who
> helps us has cleared the roof from a heavy snow
> and left again.
> Then    would it    still   be
> better   outside   alone,   only outside?

## Relating

Are you a young ant or
a small one?
diligently bent for
somewhere, at any rate.

                And do you wonder
about your place under the huge
invisibly starry sky
this July morning —

                as I do mine?


The being of an ant
must mark itself,
an alive being, intricately
impelled to run along like that, at least —
with more segmented strange
awarenesses, beyond
this other living creature's grasp.


Many speak languages
I've never learned.
Is your being one
pictograph, seed of a
word, the gateway to
a language nobody speaks?
So none can read this

unsegmented, unsmall,
shared reality.

The radii of power
are focused down and in
on you and me over our
warped little shadows; they
adjust, this midday instant, to
us, moving.

I greet you on your way.
You greet me too, departing?

## Responses

No brilliant sun as earlier when beside the
railing (it had seemed
almost possible for the shadow of me
to ride away on the
shadow of the parked bicycle).

No wind.

These listening leaves
quiet me who am all
eyes; even the dangling
leaves on the young trees listen.
I lean my hand
on the rough bark of the
deepest. It's scarcely cupped
around the ageless ample girth.
My forces gather up like an
athlete's alertness. I am straining to ... hear?

With me, it's tenseness,
apprehension, or
anticipation. But the listening
leaves are easy with it.

Reluctantly, I
move on.

# Audrey: a Posthumous Portrait

*He moste needs walke in woode*
*that may not walke in towne.*
                                    *The Tale of Gamelyn*

Brisk, between musings in
the enchanted forests which
she knows exist for the dead-eyed
lords of the hunt, but whom
she indulges anyway and
for her own purposes —

> out for the hunted there
> not to protect but to continue to
> witness that they all have a chance
>                                    anyhow.

Has its magnificence — even,
at random, magnanimity.

Does not however
quite fail to preclude
the dreamer in the wood
feeling the hounds' breath on her
bare calves, before the
green chaos of the forest lofts
(is it by now rainforest?)
becomes new cover.

Remembers that
sustenance is from the forest floor.
Wind-swept up there, then
briskly, though not unaware of
perils, crackling, thuds
all the way down again.
On into town, who may not walk
          in town.

# Reversing a Crater

A scrawny old old man
(scarred, bowed down, hounded by
uniformed officials and
safe people afraid to meet his eye)
(was he possibly
a fugitive? certainly in seclusion he
sometimes nonetheless
had friends who came with food
and hoped to hear him rise and toast the king!)

that old old man
wrote me a letter.
How it found its way though
from the last-ditch,
vigilant custody,
and by how many hands,
I cannot grasp. And yet it
has found its way, long afterwards,
to this unlikely megalopolis.

Now I am also aged
in as peculiar a community
as his there must have been.

More than my eighty years had
wracked his bones.

Yet he writes
forceful and drastic words with
the clarity of sealight over high
sheltering shores.

> *Suppose that chunk, that crater-gouging*
> *comet collides with us,*
> *will you say then — with him in his extremity —*
> *'The tide of joy, never at ebb, still*
> *surges through us too towards*
> *new coasts, a new completedness'?*

What he said, so say I.

## Third Hand, First Hand

The whispers Thomas heard
walled him in with thought,
heart-sick, tormented, not
open to silly words.

Flesh to dead body. Then how
alive — and walking, here?
(He faced the brute facts more
than the ten others. He knew.)

Blind in his mirrory grief,
stony, he came to them. And
they heard "Stretch out your hand...."
Thomas abandoned proof.

They saw because they wanted to?
They all half-doubted when
He asked for fish and honeycomb,
took it, and ate it too.

      It was the doctor later who
      said it had been so.

# Notes from Dr. Carson's Exposition of I John 5

He takes us into
Him-[selfless]-self
for saving from
what dazed and distracts us
as each preoccupied
and swarming lonelily
is out for his own for one
already fading day.

Why?
Is it the way to

                                  pure

                    delight?

(The very opposite
of what we thought?

                              or not,

we think, fitting for us
as we, ourselves, not His self
would trust)?

# He Was There
## He Was Here


A whiskered mask was all I saw
in the milkers' twilight hour
of the glimmery ghost of Fortinbras
not in Denmark, but here.
Wings creaked, deep before daybreak
and flapped, bird-necks astretch,
out beyond sight in the ghoul-light
(straw-smell, wet armour-brass).

The whiskery glint was gone.
Nobody passed by the smoking glass
of the lost lake either, that morn.

Where he had gone, whom he had seen,
indeed what he might have wanted,
invisibly wired the hours between
wharf and the usual noon canteen,
but it made both disjointed.

As the day wears on, those shinbone greaves
and that bale-bright glaring no-one believes,
nor the milkwarm farm he haunted.

## Remembering Gordon G. Nanos

Visual memory:
A narrow, uninsistently
dapper "senior,"
felt hat, casual jacket
unassertive,
quietly walking, listening
(usually the companion
was the same lady);

this Residence
has its own Armistice Day
service: Nanos (air force),
with one (army) Major, two
engineering corps men
several nurses etc.,
in the front row, all — old. All standing,
painfully or not,
rigidly upright for
the national anthem.

At a Families' Day
picnic pool
in some hostess's
grassy back yard. Most adults
trying not to slump

in shiny patio furniture
observed, smiling to see
splashers and little dancers in the sun.

Nanos? He'd slipped away;
nobody had noticed
his little satchel.
The costume, when he appeared!!
In swimsuits, dripping still, gathered
the children, all aglow,
enchanted by his nods and capers
marvelling at his magic.

Nanos is gone
after four-score years. I see
a clown's death has
a spacious dignity.

# Other Oceans

1. ON

When the convulsive earth
arched under the sea
its craggy ribs were
blurted out where reefs had been
into the golden warmth for a
fraction of a second of the one
day that's a thousand years.
In the same breath, on what was risen up
swarms of wee morsels mightier than
seafoam, rockface, under weather
brought what had emerged to be
grasses of the field
breathing that sun-washed sky.
On the face of the earth
trees and tiny Arctic flowers
face upwards; animals
with velvet paws, or hoofs,
all seem to look away towards the
falling-away edge of the earth.
My face, among these others,
ours, are not as though
among these others.

## 2. WITHIN

Studies by night. By day
blinks at the intricate
script of the world. A levelling
fuzzy peach morning-light
blurs what it would
make plain. Not
soundlessly. Whirrings.
Faint sighs. Intrudes
the throb of self selecting self
out of what was suggestive of a
singing part. Unravels
some syllables of the music, in

withdrawing again.
Waits. Cannot not be expressed
but in some foreign idiom
that seems fitting although
unspoken.
   Waits
unscrolling somewhat
lop-sidedly from
the effort of withholding
intrusion. Tense. Welcomes
the night's return, and sleep.

## 3. Under

A morning triangle of shadow
divides this field. On three
sides the building bulks.
A glimmering mesh of some
impenetrable composite substance
seals in the fourth. The grass-blades
are metal tongues, so hinged
that two or three persons, let out
under the pitiless sky
for daily exercise,
can shuffle through it,
or wade, or clatter and kick
as competency or their residual
savagery permits.
These little metal grass-blades
are mathematically precise
like tree-trunks in a forested
field in France.

Somewhere the warden
sits, nettled by the clicking
of footsteps in the field,
or yard.

People outside
steel themselves to resist
any convulsive surge to storm
this new Bastille.
Nobody seems to know

why some are in there, some,

less contained, out here.
Only a scattering
at any one time stand, and then
move on across their own
shadows in the wide courtyard.

Remember, even food and drink
turned into metal. Then it was gold,
under a Midas touch that menaces
and unmakes
heroes and revolutionaries.

People's singular sense of things
is everywhere too private
(or too pre-arranged)
for any foreseeable action but
perseverance only.

The skies will ember into the
deep darkness of another
night, and sleep —
that chrysalis of waking.


4. WHEN

"O God, God of all flesh...," *


supreme artist, originator
of all designs, who sees:
for us the entering in
is long deferred, while
   "praise" in our tongue
   is merged with "price" —
   (could we go back to "laud", or
   that other word from
   "loben",
   instead?)
Far off is that horizon
of calm and contained
joy that are wholly
unselfconscious, simple,
lovely. Where is the holy

*the cry of Moses and Aaron over Korah et al.

vanishing-point
where life began and daily may
bring us alive
again? Is this
being alive?
The far off isn't, and is all
that is.


5. WHERE

Hard-edged day time does
usually recur. Same glare,
same silent
engrossing shadow.
The park is lifting up
bare branches in bouquets.
One, shafted by the sun, offers its small
flambeau. Wires
tangle underfoot and would entangle.
This place seems unfrequented.
But specks like filings
move (tilted, trickling?) (alive!)
on a dry root.

Oak trees rustle
for long months, driving
their roots down still.

6. OUT

Though helpless, here,
whoever cried out and was heard
in darkness, in quietness,
is charged:
stand; wait here,
for some lame stumbler, for
random young shufflers,
        for skyfall.
Stand, day in, day out,
readied for day upon day.

ह≫

The frozen sheets
after we fetched them in
crackled as we folded them
for propping, splayed
out on the wooden racks
in the back kitchen.

Icy sunlight gleamed
on the waxed kitchen floor.
Down went a pair of brooms
criss-cross.
"This is the sword dance!"
and Katie showed me,
leaping and flashing. Note
this was not bonny Sco'land, it was
a lowering prairie 2 p.m. and at a
scourging 40 below!


ટ્ર


At first light, on a
certain day, someone appeared, bearing
a floor-piece on his shoulders.
Its underside was flat; the other side
had wooden cleats between the wooden slats.
When he laid it level, and inside there,
you saw its wood was sun-bleached.

Nobody saw how he got in!

The old hinged metal tongues that were the
grass-blades were on a level other than
where he now steadily walked

towards the little exit-entrance doorway to
this exercise yard or punishment area.

We numbly witnessed as
a hissing skirt of fire swept
under and around
him and his platform. An air hose
soon restored the metal grass.

The solitary, once again
emerged to pace as every clicking day
they did.

Among the young, some spoke
secretly hoping to turn
their hero's grisly defeat into some
concerted attempt,
maybe more
influential and more daunting, to
unearth the incarcerator of
so many, singly — and
then to get word back, to stir up
recruits, to reconnoitre
deeper into the
secret power and the source of power.

Among the older, worn by day
upon hypnotic day,
the hope was hope for stamina
not for success, and for
courage for those more able.

"O God, God of all flesh!"

Behold the immured, the lost champion,
the dangerously young,
and us who merely persevere
along the borders of
the always unthinkable!

7. AFTER

Post-modern:

i.e. those who (he said)
in honesty of heart
deny any eternal verities; being
searchers for plausible
truth, they humbly
substitute for the old symbols,
what they affirm as
"the logocentric."

You know their thoughtful
responsible faces, their
capacity for goodness, their
willingness to show
good will.
They shoulder only their part of the
burden of living as a
matter of course.

Who can help warmly
appreciating such people
among us, leaders of thought,
careful, and when necessary, bold
in action?

How different it would be, today, to
"take up your cross and follow Me", to
"take My yoke upon you, learn…."
Take both? Take what's to hand? Find
one follows the other? or find the same bewildering
burden?

It makes no sense today
to talk this way, nor did
in A.D. 30, thereabouts.
No, but once heard it condenses

somehow. Cautions. Compels — can
flood a person, earth and sea and sky — all that
originated in a like
mystery (all who will die from
this reasonable lifetime we have known) —
with one
overwhelming focus,
for what remains of your
lifetime's doings and responsibilities,
held by a steadying pulse.

And whether some finally
together break out 'til
the stars fall, or
a sudden global change
freezes inhabitants' pulses

> one artist who, in one
> impulse once called out, from surging
> waters and fires and molten
> rock
> our earth, our little lives,

> maintains, Himself, the
> no longer appearing
> structures.

## The Whole Story

Behind that stone before
it was rolled away
a corpse lay.
There lay all I deplore:
fear, truculence — much more
that to any other I need not say.
But behind that stone I must be sure
of deadness, to allay
self-doubt, i.e. so nearly to ignore
the love and sacrifice for our
release; to nearly stray
back into the old
pursuit of virtue.

Once it is clear
it was a corpse that day,
then, then, we know the glory
of the clean place, the floor
of rock, those linens, know the hour
of His inexplicable "Peace;" the pour
— after He went away —
of wonder, readiness, simplicity,
given.

# Cycle of Community

Mid-morning paraffin film over the
dayshine has
incidentally opened the ear
to little clanks and whirrs
out there, the hum
of a world going on,
untroubled by the silent witness, sky.
We here are silent. Yet being
drawn into, with, each
creature, each machine-work
thump, each step, faraway bark,
buzz, whine, rustle, etc.
goes to give our city
a voice, dampered by distance;
serves, through outer
windless openness of skywash, to
open a bud of tremulous hearing.

Full day will blare away
later. Then —
walk (an even pace) where cars, trucks, a
cement-mixer, teenagers out of school,
and a tied puppy keening
outside the grocer's,

provide a mix the studios would
take pride in.
Go steadily for your sake and
the others' on the sidewalk
burrowing by. And keep your face
like anyone's, in
pedestrious preoccupation —
although
you'll have to part your lips
a little, to play in.
First, test the pitch of the
prevailing din
(humming), then (still with no
perceptible opening of the mouth)
intone on the same tone-level
with all the enveloping street-sound.
Louder. As loudly as you can!

Nobody hears a thing,
                    even yourself!
Otherwise surely someone would
give that quick glance of
furtive avoidance that flicks
some flushed and angrily
gesturing man you may

hear shouting along
anywhere about town. He chooses
to stray apart from the
condemnable crazy world.

Surprisingly, evening, after the hours
of sharp light, closes in
overcast. Our thunderous busynesses
shift into calmer surge and flow.
Before dark (sky and windows
contemplating emptiness) we half-
hear the foghorn and remember
the lake, and night.

## Seriously?

*Chaos* means ... "gape"!

It does?

Look up the derivation!
"Utter confusion" is just
dragged in by connotation
with the dreaded Abyss.
"Old night"\* is now all wizened.
The new cosmography says
maybe even the bottomless isn't!

Murky and ennui-ridden
is the malodorous midden
earth has become.  But it soon will be gone
down — in a "yawn"!

\*Milton's phrase

50

# Dead Ends

The dead end that I dreaded
confronts me in this
true statement!

It's apt, manageable, but
valid only in its locked cabinet.
There's no finality out here: a sphere
too vast, too growthful, too
mischievous; subject as well
to swellings, violent
combustion, whizzings off
along the light-years.

There's too much
of us for us to know.
But closing heart, and ear
is a terminus I
fear, too.
        We slam
into it, often, though knowing is a peril
almost as terrible as
never being sure
where
the dead end will
appear.

# Prospecting

There is a node. There, one day,
all ways will
swiftly converge.

    Evening's, or morning-
    star glimmers from dear old —
    too old now — burlap earth-skies.

    Behold the abandoned
    once historied
    home of us people.

Our present
orbital rush singles out some
veering.
Plumblines occur.

    (Abandoned? no,
    not yet quite smouldered out within
    a few of us.)

All waves
(once ear and eye and intuition's
and science's) wash into
symphonic silence.

Time, too.

For at the node
all energies become
that unrewarded effortless and
ruthless kindness,
Person.

## Lament for Byways

The harrowed city
swirls with grit;
it's thundery
with chutes emitting
shards, broken stone
from in behind
brickwork going, gone
to dust within.
New little canopies
appear. Wooden partitions
shield the passerby
from inward operations
(something else under the wrecker,
shovel, and scoop...). Through spy-
holed fences, we inspect
the backs of streets we knew
before.

Some starts should not be
stopped at a dead-end.
This habitual short-cut ought to
open on my old friend
the boarded-up, blue, disused
warehouse, well known to me.
Here where it stood is — just a
pavement! and empty sky!

With the old short-cut in mind
will we bear with it, white and flat?
Somehow the cars keep blinding
the last few alleys we had.

These handsome new high-rises
help us to overlook
throbbing cement-truck noises
and gritty slime underfoot.
Yesterday's old blue eyesore is
now a new tidied-up site,

but, my city, it's still in your lanes and mews
that your heart beats.

# Rising Dust

The physiologist says I am well over
half water.
I feel, look, solid; am
though leaky firm.
Yet I am composed
largely of water.
How the composer turned us out
this way, even the learned few do not
explain. That's life.

And we're in need of
more water, over and over, repeatedly
thirsty, and unclean.

The body of this earth
has water under it and
over, from
where the long winds sough
tirelessly over water, or shriek around
curved distances of ice.

Sky and earth invisibly
breathe skyfuls of
water, visible when it
finds its own level.

Even in me?
Kin to waterfalls
and glacial lakes and sloughs
and all that flows and surges,
yet I go steadily,
or without distillation climb at will
(until a dissolution
nobody anticipates).

I'm something else besides.
The biochemist does not
concern himself with this.
It too seems substance,
a vital bond threaded on an
as-if loom out there.
The strand within
thrums and shudders and twists.
It cleaves to this
colour or texture and
singles out to a rhythm
almost its own, again,
anticipating design.

But never any of us
physiologist or fisherman

or I
quite makes sense of it. We
find our own level

as prairie, auburn or
snow-streaming, sounds forever
the almost limitless.

## Two

Trees breathe for any
who breathe to live.

Stone makes every thing
more what it is:
sun-hot,

late November bare,
cold in an early April morning;

age in being
always.

## Leading Questions

Walking naked in Eden, they
lived always in the light
of the holy. Drawn to disobey
they awoke to shame — and God-

like comprehension of pain,
of broken as well as good.
(What would *our* choice have been
if we had understood?)

And what was the shame about?
And why did He need, then,
to "clothe the lilies...", who night-
ly met those unclad in Eden?

Had nakedness not meant freedom?
At evening, now forsaken
by our choice, was that to Him
as since to us, heartbreaking?

Yet He taught the Jews to weave
rich fabrics for the abode
He would live in, or above
in fire or (covering) cloud,

and long since He has promised to prepare
for us the robe He hopes His guests that Day will wear.

## Uncircular

The entombment of all that wrath
bespeaks the stench of a
fragmenting into
finality.
To me, this matters.
I anchor there as to a lifeline,

ৰ৯

there where
what other self-bound persons
had wrapped and lovingly
laid, a total
loss for all, for all
was found in purity, among his friends
changed, but the same time opening
everything on earth to the
power that lifted him.

No wonder Paul cried out,
"I count all loss…" — above all, loss.

ৰ৯ ৰ৯ ৰ৯

Among us, Jesus found
encrusted words and structures;
he washed and brushed them clean
and out of the intractability
of history learned by rote
stepped, in simplicity the exemplar,

into the prairies of
dutiful days, each with the taste
of moving slowly towards...without
the horizon coming any closer.

His are the evenings of a
king in a cave kept wakeful by
deftly deciphering the
poems he found written in his heart.

When most of his people trailed
about in molting plumage —
aping, through fear and envy,
those not themselves —
he brokenheartedly
tried to put heart in them
again, or rouse them to the dread, in time,

that dragged them down
into insensibility.

In the besieged city
he moved among the panic-crazed;
and where skin-and-bone
cannibals crept or
by the walls, rocked against the rock
like a cribbed infant.
Once for a time
all of them were
strangers far from home.
They knew the wreckage to be
faced and put together somehow
on their return some day.

Once again there, Jesus too found
words twisted, rubble about, and
again he swept and tended them
gently, almost smiling
when some who so cherished
the traditional that they urged
stains, gritty particles, dust
must be left, too, untouched.

His words flowed from a
clear wellspring always 'til now
a little tainted by the
hand that cupped to drink, or the
crafted ladle.

Why was this one then
dragged off and left abandoned to
indifferent cruelty once, with no
home left, anywhere?

219

Entombment, however, is
new in all history.
What it is for.

# The Endangerer

Swept in among the wave-suds,
moved gently out, and in,
flotsam, he lay, a log
to any shorewalker.
And one approached. He always came
at sundown.

Alive still? Yes!
The rescue crew he brought
churned up the shore, so that the slant sun
made a lengthening shadow behind
every clump, a dot at every grain.

Today, erect, the stranger
strolls past his unremembered
couch among the
shell-chips and weedy runnels.

And there before him, prone,
the swelling waters brim,
benign, bemusing:
"This watery world is flat, and every wavelet
is a homecoming from the bourne."

It had taken a further journey for the
convalescent to
frame — and paint out — the lie.

# To Wilfred Cantwell Smith

*When asked, What is an intellectual? he said:*
*"An intellectual is a participant in his own*
*society, listening to people. That kind of truth*
*cannot be put anywhere by us, not in words, never*
*put in its place. The human mind can apprehend,*
*not comprehend."*

Our native language shapes us, does it not
even as it shapes itself upon the page?
The languages you've learned, in life and college,
carve and emboss characters in your thought?

Hebrew's ornate iron, its quirks around the line
(vocal or consonant) in you have wrought
the odd intransigent openness — and untaught
much we grew up to mimic — or disdain.

Myopic, skeptical, sometimes distraught,
slowly your readers see ourselves as foreign,
trotting for safety through our little warren
of walled ways. Now, perilously, we're out

in a big world of foreigners, finding that they are not!
Ink on white paper keeps informing those
who learn, to listen long, until there glows
within the friendly signs of being understood.

Urdu's visual/inner shapes I've not

seen on the page to see in you. I know
Persian and Arabic's fluid music though
(to the eye); which to your nature also brought

a spare poetry. Such surprises dot
and wink away through universal
(meticulously measurable)
spaces, and what's been sought
within shines there, articulate, through the night.

# Four Words

*Revealed*
The other has confronted,
touched on the quick, borne with through
awful combative silence — almost
inaction — until knowing one is
known, now.

*Knowing*
One is the observer of,
made participant in,
momentarily
caught, stilled;
listens with every fibre;
and to the swiftly far away
vanishing, an unpursuer
humbled.

*Prophecy*
Words are
imparted, able to calm,
quick to wrestle – and best;
they map a long long travelling
beyond experience even.

*Teaching*
Small exaltations of spirit demand

groundedness. Now too long
past dawn it's time to get down to
listening, learn to talk too
without interference from
yourself, doing what's been
given to be done.


(A gloss on I Cor. 14:6)

## On a Maundy Thursday Walk

The Creator was
walking by the sea, the
Holy Book says. Finely-tuned
senses — flooded with
intense awareness — tested
a clear serene constancy.

Who can imagine it, sullied
as our senses are? Faulty as are even our
most excellent makings?

The perfection of
created Being, in the perfect
morning was born from the walker-by-the-sea's
imagination. At a word —
the hot smell of sunned rock, of
the sea, the sea, the sound of lapping, bird-calls,
the sifting sponginess of sand
under the sandals, delicate.
April light — all, at a word
had become this almost-
overwhelming loveliness.

Surely the exultation —
the Artist
Himself immersed in

His work, finding it flawless —
intensified the so soon
leaving (lifted out of
mortal life for good
forever).

That too eludes
us who disbelieve that we
also shall say goodbye to
trees and cherished friends and
sunsets and crunching snow
to travel off
into a solo death.

How much more, that
(suffering this
creation to go under
its Maker, and us all)
He, the Father of love, should stake it all
on a sufficient
indeed on an essential
pivot.

# In our "little nests"

To freely write or say
what may give offence
is finding one's not free
or — was, at great expense.

Tuttuttery today
fits politics. The ones
who judged censoriously
in opposition once

when their party prevails
in power, discover why
solutions will entail
the problems they decry.

One set on sensibly
pricking ballooning notions
before they ride too high
flattens some fond illusions.

After the hullabaloo
what will be assessed?
Whose thinking will come through
as troublesome — at best?

જ

Meaning no harm is nice since

it's seeing no harm really.
Who cares? It provides licence
to speak out freely.

# Contextualizing, or Neither Here nor There

To "hate those who hate You" —
or you —
(rather than those who may be
     out and out down on me)
seems a moral necessity
encompassed in
     "loving our enemies."

                    Out here
there's an unconscious undertone
of fond contempt, at best,
when anyone adverts to what
once mattered so much
to other shapers of
style, in opinion. Here
cuttings from the hothouses
 (where yesterday's flowers of the field are
coaxed to limp survival)
are cherished as new rank
growth, for general benefit out here
— without embarrassment
of wormy soil, or festering, or
composting at the end perhaps.

                    Inside
there comes sick longing to be out from under
shelter in the bald day,

even to wither there.

                                   Out here
with hate, loving, it can too soon
begin to seem
cool, that "shadow of turning."


                                   Inside
it's harder still to sidestep
minimal, chilling compromises —
too little respecting, or
too defensive about our
amazing range of individualities
under the one rubric that matters.

## Alternative to Riots
## but All Citizens Must Play

To myself everywhere:
Cry out, "Break!" Break
all our securities, and break out!
Explore only the ranges
beyond our mastering. Take on
the inexorable demands made by
a norm of unpremeditated excellence!

ે&

Forget the elegant speeches,
the unbreakable delicacy
or cello resonance of
"art". Forget
faceless, imperial (world-wide)
governance and its shimmery
statistical sheen. Why,
even the memory-traces of
classical Greece's music are
long forgotten. (The Empire then was Rome's.)

Our own skills and
achievements are imprisoned by
managed relationships

no-one can manage, quite.
Money we used to see,
in metal baubles, jig along the wires.*
Money is no longer
visible. Now
it vapourizes and disperses somehow
and settles over all of us.
We turn into a monstrous
sameness, a jumble
within one skin,
a skin pulled taut
until it hurts
the whole ungeographical
world of us.

       * Back when the new technology
         was electricity,
         the first department stores were
         festooned with maypole-radiating wires.
         The dancers' ends came down to
         clerks parcelling purchases.
         The money offered and the invoices
         were stuffed in metal baubles and sent off
         jigging up the wires
         to the store's one
         change-maker, stamper of receipts,
         set apart up on a
         mezzanine level, caged
         but always in plain view.

Break out! Break from all safe
comprehensive arrangements
never completely comprehended by
controllers or controlled.
Once there were landscapes, features,
rugged outcroppings, signatures
bespeaking persons. Now they all melt into
categories, till conglomeration
begins to make categories
a fiction, although still
a soothing one.
Security shackles us in shame and helplessness; the
insecure are bony; they
shuffle past, lean
anywhere, drained clean of
expecting, or of anything
beyond the courage to go on
dully surviving.

Beware of any notion of
safety from having clustered under
some forced, or chosen,
minority. All of them are
self-centred, all a
security that blinds and deafens
exposing flank, and heart

to poisons from within as well.
Where can anyone find
sanctuary, now that
lethal puffs drift
out of a fair sky,
drift down?
Gunshot crackles in the
streets after our sheltering
walls have crumpled.
And still the illustrious ones, the
conference diplomats, the key
negotiators — a unique
minority — are
emperors on parade,
unaware of being not even
clad let alone cloaked.

Some count on the majority
out there, bland in its
openness, our security in
the social swim. But like so many sure
foundations, latterly, this one
seems unsettlingly wobbly.
The animus keeps fading into

passivity. Many that were
supports, happily tolerating
anything — almost — now
lean, to imbalance, straggling off.
Stop them! Disrupt these
vanilla visions, spongy with
yearnings, for prophesied
pre-dawn light, this very day.

Nightfall is near.

Break in! Break up
all our so solid structures for the
glory of
nothing to hold onto
but untried air currents,
the crack and ricochet
of impact. Risk
survival! into
some indestructible
transmuted loss. There will begin,
perhaps, a slow
secret, gradual, germinating
in the darkness.

# Notes

p. 15 "Prairie Poem: for George Grant". George Grant (1918-1988), worked in Adult Education, then after study abroad he became a university teacher, latterly at Dalhousie. He wrote *Philosophy in the Mass Age*, *Lament for a Nation*, *Technology and Justice*, etc. etc.

We became friends in Toronto, when George came to recuperate from TB, after duties during the London Blitz. His courage in wartime England as a pacifist was impressive. Later, when studies and teaching took him to other cities, his articles and books kept me in touch. Two writers central to me, Dostoyevsky and Jacques Ellul, cropped up in George's writings. We met again in his York University-McMaster period, when his rambunctious but principled consistency delighted me. George worked under a sky that kept opening out.

p. 30 "Notes from Dr. Carson's Exposition of I John 5". Donald A. Carson is a Canadian theologian, presently Research Professor of New Testament, Trinity Evangelical Divinity School, Deerfield, Illinois. This poem refers to a sermon he gave in Toronto.

p. 67 "To Wilfred Cantwell Smith". Wilfred Cantwell Smith (1916-1999), was introduced to Canadian readers in 1962 by the published CBC series *The Faith of Other Men*. His last two books, in 1998, are *Patterns of Faith around the World* and *Faith and Belief.* Reference works call him an "Islamicist" – see his *On Understanding Islam*, 1984. He taught at McGill, Dalhousie, and, for the last years, as Professor of Comparative Religion at Harvard.

In failing health, he and his wife moved to the seniors' residence where I live. The in-house paper delegated me to interview him simply as a new resident. The Smiths' friendly, unassuming welcome made it easy, although I was awed to learn that Wilfred spoke Urdu, Arabic, and many European languages, and his wife (a surgeon who practiced in India before Partition) spoke Punjabi and some oriental languages as well. Until their health forced a move to nursing care, I had the joy of reading aloud (his sight was increasingly poor) many an afternoon, with breaks for conversation. The epigraph records one comment he made in passing!

# Acknowledgements

Thank you to Maggie Helwig of *The Canadian Forum*, Barry Callaghan of *Exile*, Gregory Wolfe of *Image* (Spokane, WA.), and Chuck Congram of *The Presbyterian Record*, for helping my poems to reach readers.

To Brick Books, who kept my previous books available after Lancelot Press closed, my ongoing thanks too.

Since I discarded a computer, hand-written manuscripts kept accumulating. Joan Eichner, who had long been a responsive reader, encouraged me to gather them, and let her put them on computer.

From *No Time* on, Joan would scrutinize what I began to see as first or second drafts. Her questions, her spotting of unintended ambiguities, her fine ear for syntax, helped clear away superfluous difficulties; and she never intruded when I declared a text must stand. Such invaluable help I want to acknowledge here.

Stan Dragland's meticulous and responsive editing, in preparing the final text, deserves special mention, as does Maureen Harris's careful technical work in preparing the manuscript for printing.

Margaret Avison

M argaret Avison was born in Galt, Ontario. She attended public school in western Canada, high school and university in Toronto. Her first book, *Winter Sun*, won the Governor General's Award for Poetry, as did *No Time* (1989). She holds three honorary doctorates and is an officer of the Order of Canada. *A Kind of Perseverance* (her 1993 Pascal Lectures at the University of Waterloo) was published in 1994.